Criptionary

Disability Humor & Satire

by

Maria R. Palacios

Atahualpa Press
Houston, Texas

Library of Congress Number   2013921206
Palacios Maria R. 2013
Criptionary –Disability Humor and Satire

   I.   Title

ISBN 978-0-9726483-1-8

For John Callahan whose crip humor inspires my own.

As a person with a disability, and especially as a writer with a disability, I take pride in the birth of this collection of words through which disability culture manifests itself to the able-bodied world. Criptionary is my personal way of redefining disability through the power of humor while still maintaining a sharp edge of the realities we face day to day.

–Maria R. Palacios

A special thanks to my dear friend Teresa Biggar whose loving support gave this book that dictionary flavor to it.

Also with appreciation I want to acknowledge my friend Julie Prough whose enthusiasm and love for this project helped make it a reality.

Foreword
By Mat Fraser

Criptionary is a new tome of Crip-related re-worded definitions by Maria Palacios, a disabled wordsmith who displays great wit, passion, humor, sexuality, irreverence, good and bad taste gags, in this thought provoking, and hugely entertaining book. Though perhaps initially for a niche market, I think anyone reading it would be amused and find themselves further critiquing our language.

Much of this book is as much silly as it is serious. But even the silly stuff has a serious aftermath for it forces the reader to consider the issue raised in the word's meaning, and therefore explodes so many of the negative myths and clichés around disability that still linger in society. Virtually every word brings forth an interlocking of thought pattern, confused at times by the imaginative re wording, spurred on at others to appreciate the cleverness with which she has constructed some words from others, and her commitment to bringing crip love and stories to the World through this witty method of a brand new dictionary for Crip prism living, which shines out on every page.

Speaking as a **CripRex** ("known for their abnormally short arms." That's me! - I'm also "**Cripendowed**", so there - No, buy the book and look it up for yourself) I can say that you don't have to suffer from being a **Cripevert** ("According to Society, anybody who finds a disabled person sexually attractive") to think this book is worth having and using for all manner of moments, and could get you singing **Criptanamera** ("popular crip Latin song") for joy.

Mat Fraser   -Actor, writer, comedian & activist/multi disciplinary performing disability artist

Criptionary

Disability Humor & Satire

Maria R. Palacios

Crip-A

Crip-A

Crip /krɪp/: person with a disability

crip-a-tab /krɪpˈeɪ·tæb /: to educate a TAB /Temporarily Able-Bodied about crip culture

crip-ass /krɪpˈæs /: a disabled donkey

cripa'int /krɪp-eɪ ˈɪnt /: improper way of saying "I'm not disabled."

cripabilities /krɪpˈə·bɪl·ɪ·ţiz /: the unique abilities of crips

crip-aboo /krɪpˈeɪ·bu /: a disabled parent playing peek-a-boo with an infant

cripabsurdity /kripəbˈzɜ:.dɪ.ti/: some people's assumption that crips with similar disabilities are automatically aware of one another despite never having met or heard of each other

cripaccent /krɪpˈæk·sent /: the way people with CP sound

cripacity /krɪpˈæs.ə.ti /: a crip's capacity to tolerate society's stupidity

cripacolada /krɪpˈkoʊ·lə·dɑ /: a crip who has gotten drunk on pina coladas

cripadise /krɪpˈəˌdɑɪs /: accessible vacation resort

crip-a-fuck /krip.a fʌk/: crips' way of saying "I don't care"

cripaid /krɪpˈeɪd /: crip flavored drink

cripaltruism /krip/ˈæl.tru.ɪ.zəm/: crips who share their modest means with an able-bodied person who can do more than them

cripamnesia /krɪpˈæm·ni·ʒə /: what makes some crips forget about others like them when climbing up the ladder of crip success

cripanalogy /krɪpˈə·næl·ə·dʒi /: some people's habit of thinking all disabilities are the same

Cripanese /krɪpˈə·niːz /: a Japanese crip

cripangelic /krɪpˈæn·dʒel·ɪk /: a crip who looks very innocent but isn't

cripanalysis /kripəˈnæl.ə.sɪs/: the habit of thinking that when crips are in a bad mood, it is because they're bitter about being disabled

cripanholic /krɪpˈæn·hɔ·lɪk /: sadness experienced by a crip when remembering the able-bodied days

cripanonymous /krɪpˈə·nɑn·ə·məs /: person who tries to hide his or her disability

crippappeal /krɪpˈə·piːl /: curb appeal of accessible homes

cripappetite /krip/ˈæp.ɪ.taɪt/: what crips say to a lover who is providing oral pleasuring

cripapple /krɪpˈæp·əl /: the forbidden apple after it was bitten

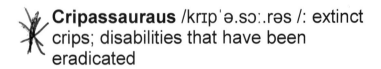

Cripassauraus /krɪpˈə·sɔː.rəs /: extinct crips; disabilities that have been eradicated

cripastrophic /krɪpˈæs·trə·fɪk /: wheelchair flat tire

cripastures /krɪpˈæs·tʃərs /: where disabled horses go when they retire

Cripasutra /krɪp-əˈsuː. trə /: the Kamasutra for crips

cripathon /krɪpˈəˌθɑn /: the Jerry Lewis Telethon

cripathy /krɪpˈə.θi /: society's apathy towards disabled people

cripativity /krɪpˈeɪ·tɪv·ɪ·t̬i /: a crip's energy of creativity

cripattention /krɪpˈəˈten·ʃən /: the silence that fills a room when a crip takes the stage

cripattude /krɪpˈæt.tjuːd /: positive attitude about one's disability

cripauguration /krɪpˈɔg·jəˌre·ʃən /: inauguration of an agency that serves the disabled but is overseen by nondisabled folks

crip-aversion-therapy /krip əˈvɜː-ʒən er.ə.pi /: historical electroshock treatment of persons with mental illness

cripawakening /krɪpˈ əˈweɪ·kənɪŋ/: crips' realization that they're still whole even if their body isn't

Cripazoid /krɪpˈə.zɔɪd /: evil twin of the Super Crip

Crip B-C

Crip B-C

cripbackriding /krɪpˈbæk·rɑɪ·dɪŋ /: crips' version of doggie style

Cripback Mountain /krɪpbæk maʊn.tɪn /: Award winning documentary detailing the struggles and challenges faced by a crip gay couple

cripband-aid /krip ˈbænd.eɪd /: society's habit of trying to solve disability related problems by covering them up with incomplete and temporary solutions

cripberry /krɪpˈber·i /: phone with specially created accessibility apps

crip's best friend /krip /best /frend/ : a service animal

cripbigotry /kripˈbɪg.ə.tr/: some crips' tendency to reject being part of the crip community but take full advantage of disability services and rights covered under the law

cripbits /krɪp bɪt/: Little People

cripbites /krip baɪts/ : little people with an attitude

cripbloid /krɪpˈblɔɪd /: crip publication about the latest gossip in the crip community

cripbones /krɪpˈboʊns /: crips way of referring to dominoes

cripbotics /krɪpˈbɑt̬·ɪks /: the making of bionic limbs

cripboundary /krɪpˈbaʊn·dri /: the socially imposed ignorance those with disabilities must overcome day to day

cripbozo /krɪpbəʊ.zəʊ/: clown who entertains children with disabilities

cripbreak /krɪpˈbreɪk /: not charging anything to cash Social Security Disability checks

cripbro /krɪpˈbroʊ /: a disabled brother

cripbuffet /krɪpˈbə·feɪ /: crip beauty pageant

cripbute /krɪpˈb·jut /: tribute to an outstanding crip

crip-by-association /krip baɪ əˌsəʊ.siˈeɪ.ʃən /: able-bodied people who park in disability assigned parking spaces with a borrowed parking tag

cripbyebye /krɪpˈbaɪ·baɪ /: the passing of a crip

cripCIS /kripCIS/: agency that investigates disability related hate crimes

cripcalypso /krɪpˈkə·lɪp·soʊ /: to ask a disabled lover, "How low can you go?"

CripCam /krɪpˈkæm /: popular crip reality TV show which focuses on crip humor

cripcaracha /krɪpˈkʌ·rɑː·tʃə /: Spanish word for disabled cockroach

cripcarceration /kripˌkɑː.sərˈeɪ.ʃən/: crips serving time behind bars in inaccessible conditions

cripcard /krɪpˈkard /: a crip's medical marijuana card

cripcartel /krɪpˈkɑr·tel /: underground market of catheters sold to uninsured crips

cripcasualty /krɪpkæʒ.ju.əl.ti/: crips who fall through the cracks of the system

cripcalico /krɪp ˈkæl.ɪ.kəʊ /: crips with multiple disabilities

cripcaution /krɪpˈkɔː.ʃən /: what walking people should have around wheelchairs

cripcave /krɪpˈkeɪv /: fully disability friendly space where crips gather to chill and have fun

cripcebo /krɪpˈsi·boʊ /: the social placebo of telling those with disabilities that they don't look or act disabled

Crip-Charming /krɪpˈʃɑrmɪŋ /: the perfect crip bachelor

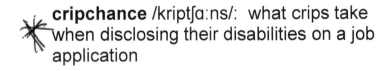

cripchance /krɪptʃɑːns/: what crips take when disclosing their disabilities on a job application

cripchat /krɪpˈtʃæt /: chatting with a crip who does not communicate through traditional methods

cripcharity /kripˈtʃær.ɪ.ti/: what society thinks it does by providing partial human rights to persons with disabilities

cripcheat /krípkrɪpˈtʃiːt /: people who request a wheelchair at the airport so they can board first

cripchef /kripʃef/: Christine Ha

cripchop /kriptʃɒp/: crip who knows karate

crip-clog /krɪpˈklɑg /: crips way of describing constipation

cripcocoa /krɪpˈkoʊ·koʊ /: a disabled black person

cripcojones /krɪpˈkoʊ·hoʊn·ɑɪs /: what some people see crips having just for living life like an average person

cripcomedian /krɪpˈkə·mid·i·ən /: person in a wheelchair who does stand up comedy

cripconciliation /krɪpˈkənˌsɪl·iˈeɪ·ʃən /: to reconcile with one's body after becoming disabled

cripcontrol /krɪpˈkən·troʊl /: a roller's ability to control his or her bladder during a long flight

cripcop /krɪpˈkɑp /: a police officer who became disabled in the line of duty

cripcopy /krɪpˈkɑp·i /: identical crip twins

cripcorn /krɪpˈ kɔrn /: popcorn kernels that didn't pop

cripcorrupt /krɪpˈkə·rʌpt /: what some would think sex education to be for people with disabilities

cripcrap /krɪpˈkræp /: a crip's bowel routine

cripcrastination /krɪpˈkræs.tɪ·neɪ.ʃən /: crips' common practice of waiting till the last minute to use the bathroom

cripcredit /krɪpˈ kred•ɪt/: some ablebodied people's sense of entitlement after experiencing a temporary disability

cripcreeping /krɪpˈkrip·ɪŋ /: a roller's attempt to sneak out of a place quietly

cripcrib /krɪpˈkrɪb /: place where young disabled people gather

cripcrispy /krip/ˈkrɪs.pi/: a crip who stayed too long in the sun

crip-crop /krɪpˈkrɑp /: the digital alteration of a crip's image to make them appear less disabled

cripcross /krɪpˈkrɔs /: to betray a crip friend

cripcuatro /krɪpˈkwɑ·troʊ /: a quad

cripcubation /krɪpˈkjʊ·beɪ·ʃən /: eggs incubated by disabled hens

cripculture /krɪpˈkʌl·tʃər /: the history, traditions, language and common causes shared by crips

cripcumcision /krɪpˈkəmˌsɪʒ·ən /: the erroneous believe that a disabled man is unable to satisfy a woman

cripcupine /krɪpˈkjəˌpaɪn /: a disabled person with a Mohawk

cripcurse /krip/kɜrs/: some cultures' belief that a disability is a punishment from God

cripcurfew /kripˈkɜː.fju/: schedule crips with significant disabilities must abide by in order to get in or out of bed

cripcurious /krɪpˈkjʊər·i·əs /: curiosity to sleep with a crip to see if it's the same as with other people

Crip D-E

Crip D-E

cripdesign /krɪpˈdɪ·zɑɪn /: the art of making accessible homes attractive to ablebodied buyers

cripdenominator /krɪpdɪˈnɒm.ɪ.neɪ.tər/: the common causes shared by crips despite the diversity of their disabilities

cripdiculous /krɪp dɪk.jʊ.ləs/: crips who benefit from government programs but vote against the continuation of such

crip-disappearance /krɪp ˌdɪs.əˈpɪə.rəns /: able-bodied people's ability to forget about the disability after seeing the person behind the label

cripdoctrinate /krɪpˈdɒk.trɪ.neɪt /: to educate a newly disabled person about crip culture and life in the crip lane.

cripdown /krɪpˈdaʊn /: a disabled person performing oral sex

cripduo /krɪp ˈdjuː.əʊ /: conjoint twins

cripduction /krɪpˈdʌk·ʃən /: when a crip seduces an ablebodied person

crip Dr.Ruth /kripdɒk.təruːθ./: crip sexologist who understands the complexity of crip sexuality and offers honest feedback regardless of socially preconceived ideas of ability

cripeloquence /kripˈel.ə.kwəns/: some crips' ability to tell people to fuck off and still be elegant and classy

cripempathy /kripˈem.pə.θi/: crips' ability to relate to one another; peer counseling

cripend /krɪpˈend /: spending your weekend with crips

Cripendella /krɪpˈənˈdel.ə /: definition of the idea that a woman with a disability is always desperately waiting for an able-bodied Prince Charming.

cripendipity /krɪp.ənˈdɪp.ɪ.ti /: the serendipity of two crips finding each other under strange and seemingly impossible circumstances

cripendowed /krɪpˈɪnˈdɑʊd /: a well-endowed crip

cripenvy /krɪpˈen·vi /: what some able-bodied people feel when a crip doesn't have to wait in line

criperstanding /krɪpˈər·stæn·dɪŋ /: honest understanding of the complexity of crips

criperstitious /krɪpˈər·stɪ·ʃəs /: the believe that that looking at a disabled person could jinx you

cripervert /krɪpˈər·vɜrt /: according to society, anybody who finds a disabled person sexually attractive

cripex /krɪpˈeks /: the way society thinks disabled people have /S /ex, as if something's missing.

cripexception /krip/ɪkˈsep.ʃən/: allowing wheelchair users to pass through airport security without going through metal detectors and x-ray machines because such are not accessible

cripexhaust /krɪpˈɪg·zɔst /: using the same crips over and over to represent an entire community of crips

cripexperts /krip /ˈek.spɜːt/ : some people's tendency to believe they know what's best for crips; the Medical Model

Crip F-G

Crip F-G

cripfabrication /krip/fæb.rɪ.keɪt/: crips with imagined disabilities; hyponchondriacs

cripfaith /krip/feɪθ/: crips' ability to believe life goes on despite disability

Crip Factor /krɪpˈfæk·tər /: a crip talent show

cripfairy /krɪpˈfeər·i /: those who think crips can be healed through prayer or magic

cripfan /krɪpˈfæn /: those who admire crips

Crip Fancy /KrɪpˈFæn·si /: a magazine for those who love crips

Cripfax /krɪpˈfæks /: ownership history when selling a used wheelchair

cripfect /krɪpˈfɪkt /: crips who feel just perfect as they are

cripfeet /krɪpˈfit /: wrinkles of wisdom that grow around the eyes of crips as they age

cripfeetunder /krɪpˈfitˌʌn·dər /: the way crips are buried when they die

cripfference /krɪpˈfrəns /: noticeable differences between crips

cripfermentation /krip/ˌfɜː.menˈteɪ.ʃən/: alcoholic crips

cripfiltrate /krɪpˈfɪl·treɪt /: the attempt to infiltrate disability awareness in the lives of non disabled folks

cripfish /krɪpˈfɪʃ /: NEMO

cripfinale /krip/fɪˈnɑː.li/: disabilities linked to a terminal illness

cripflame /krɪpˈfleɪm /: an illicit love affair between crips

cripflap /krɪpˈflæp /: the way lifeless body parts move during sex

cripflash /krɪpˈflæʃ /: short glimpse of a disabled person in a crowded place

cripflesh /krɪpˈfleʃ/: naked crip

cripflirting /kripflɜːting/: to risk rejection by insinuating intimacy with an able-bodied person

cripflix /krɪpˈflɪks/: disability related movies

cripfloat /krɪpˈfloʊt/: disabled person taking a bath

cripflock /krɪpˈflɑk/: crips of a feather flying together

cripformity /krɪpˈfɔrm·ɪ·t̪i/: to conform with social rules that violate a crip's rights to dignity

cripfraud /krɪpˈfrɔd/: to pass as a crip to receive government benefits

cripgames /krɪpˈgeɪmz/: Paralympics

cripgasm /krɪpˈgæz·əm/: mental orgasm

cripgear /krɪpˈgɪr/: cool gadgets that elegantly enhance a person's quality of mobility

cripgeeks /krɪpˈgiks /: crips whose main love is technology

cripgenius /krip ˈdʒiː.ni.əs / Stephen Hawking

cripginning /krɪpˈgɪn·ɪŋ /: the beginning of a crip's journey in a disabled body

cripGoddess /krɪpˈgɑd·əs /: Venus

cripsgonewild /kripsgɒnwaɪld/: crips who have had enough and speak up against the injustices they face when trying to assert their independence

cripguilt /krɪpˈgɪlt /: Catholic crips

Crip H-I

Crip H-I

crip-habilitation /krɪpˈhə·bɪl·ɪ·te·ʃən /: the attempt to make a crip go back to pre-crip abilities

criphanage /krɪpˈfə·nɪdʒ /: place where disabled children are abandoned

criphappens /krɪphæp.əns/: the reality that nobody is immune to becoming disabled

cripheal /krɪpˈhil /: command ablebodied people wish they could make come true

crip-heros /krɪphɪə.rəʊs/: crips whose disabilities were acquired by serving our country; disabled veterans

crip-hint /krɪpˈhɪnt /: people's way of trying to guess one's disability

criphobia /krɪpˈfoʊ·bi·ə /: fear of those with disabilities

criphobic /krɪpˈfoʊ·bɪk /: those who fear a disability is contagious or bad luck

criphoarding /krip'hɔ:.dɪŋ/: assisted living and group home facilities that overbook themselves in order to make more money

crip-hole /krɪp'hoʊl /: a crip who's an asshole

criphood /krɪp'hʊd /: segregated housing where people with disabilities live

crip-hop /krɪp'hɑp /: a one legged person

criphuevo /krɪp'huevo/: Humpty Dumpty

criphunger /krip'hʌŋ.gər/: the social inclusion craved by crips whose lives are spent in isolation

cripiatrics /krɪp·i'æ·trɪks /: doctors who treat either children or older people with disabilities

cripignite /krip/ɪg'naɪt/: to respond to a crip's sexual arousal

cripifice /krɪpˈəˌfaɪs /: the act of sacrificing the real self in the name of normality

cripilingus /krɪpˈɪ·lɪŋ.gəs /: the pleasure of orally satisfying a crip woman

cripimp /krɪpˈ ɪmp /: male crip on a purple wheelchair with a big stereo and a gold chain

cripimprinting /krip/ɪmˈprɪnting/: crips who fall in love with the first person who shows them physical affection

cripin /krɪpˈɪn /: the opposite of cripout

cripincarnation /krɪpˈɪn·karˈneɪ·ʃən /: a disabled person who acquires an additional disability later in life

cripindulgent /krip/ɪnˈdʌl.dʒənt/: crips who spend part of their fixed income on occasional pleasures such as a movie night or dinner with a friend

cripink /krɪpˈɪŋk /: tattoos on a crip

cripinn /krɪpˈɪn /: hotel or motel that offers wheelchair accessibility and disability friendly amenities

cripinsane /krɪpɪnˈseɪn/: what society things crips to be for thinking they can live independently

cripinspire /krɪp ɪnˈspaɪər/: what crips are expected to do for nondisabled folks just by going about our business in the able-bodied world

cripintentional /krɪp/ɪnˈten.ʃən.əl/: disabilities that were self-inflicted

cripintrigue /krɪp ɪnˈtriːg/: curiosity of a crip who grew up disabled about able-bodied life

cripintrovert /krɪpˈɪn.trə.vɜːt/: person with Autism

cripintrude /krɪp ɪnˈtruːd/: Some able-body people's habit of forcing help upon a crip although help was not requested

Crip-in-Shiny-Armor
/krɪpˈinˈʃaɪ·niˈɑr·mər /: crip who wears braces and /or his loyal steed is a wheelchair

cripintuition /krɪpˌɪn.tjuːˈɪʃ.ən/: a crip's ability to detect a sense of discomfort in able-bodied people

Crip J-K-L

Crip J-K-L

cripjaculation /krɪpˈdʒæk·jəˌleɪ·ʃən /: male crip's orgasm achieved in unconventional ways

cripjam /krɪpˈdʒæm /: wheelchair traffic jam

cripjoles /krɪpˈhoʊl·eɪs /: beans cooked by a Mexican crip

cripjunkies /kripdʒʌŋ.kis/: crips who become addicted to prescription drugs for which the government pays

CripKat /krɪpˈkæt /: crips' favorite candy

cripkermit /kripk kəˈrmɪt/: frogs whose legs have been taken for food

cripkissing /krɪpˈkɪs·sɪŋ /: a game of spin the bottle that does not exclude those with obvious disabilities

cripknit /krɪpˈnɪt /: the act of being close as a community between crips

CripKong /krɪpˈk ɒŋ /: disabled gorilla

criplabor /krɪpˈleɪ·bər /: the hard work it takes for crips to do just about anything

criplacio /krɪpˈleɪ·ʃi·oʊ /: oral pleasuring of a male crip lover

criplamp /krɪpˈlæmp /: magic lamp unable to produce a gini

cripland /krɪpˈlænd /: what happens when a crip falls

criplash /krɪpˈlæʃ /: a crip with a whip

criplatte /krɪpˈlɑː.t̬eɪ /: highly caffeinated crip

criplaw /krɪpˈlɑː /: the ADA

cripleague /krɪpˈliːg /: a sports league formed by crips

criplegacy /krɪpˈleg·ə·si /: the personal and collective history left by crips to the next generation

criplement /krɪpˈləˌment /: something meant as a compliment that sounds more like an insult

criplendar /krɪpˈlən·dər /: calendar of events in the disability community

cripleness /krɪp·əlˈnəs /: positive definition of crip self

cripless-fuck /krɪpˈles·fʌk /: to have sex with a non-disabled person

criplets /krɪpˈlɪts /: disabled triplets

criplevel /krip/ˈlev.əl/: to kneel in order to be at eye level with a roller or person of short stature

criplievability /krɪpˈli·və·bəl·ɪ·ti /: people who can pass as crips

criplightning /krɪpˈlaɪt·nɪŋ /: what happens when a crip gets an idea

criplingual /krɪpˈlɪŋ·gwəl /: an ablebodied person who has experience with disability lingo

criplink /krɪpˈlɪŋk /: an ablebodied person's crip friend who keeps hm/her connected with the disabled world

criplip /krɪpˈlɪp /: outspoken crip

criploan /krip ləʊn /: to borrow an able-bodied person's abilities to accomplish certain tasks

criplocate /krɪpˈloʊ·keɪt /: to find the exatc location of a crip

cripluggage /krɪpˈlʌg·ɪdʒ /: what crips' wheelchairs become when traveling

cripluptuous /krɪpˈlʌp·tʃu·əs /: disabled voluptuous woman

cripluxury /kripˈlʌk.ʃər.i/: to be able to afford home modifications after becoming disabled

cripmageddon /krɪpˈmə·ged.ən /: society's wish for a crip free world.

Crip M-N

Crip M-N

cripmanship /krɪpˈmæn·ʃɪp /: comfort level with one's crip mannerisms and presentation

cripmaintainance /kripˈmeɪn.tɪ.nəns/: to have to care for body parts that no longer agree with the rest of the body

cripmarking /krɪp ˈmɑr·kiŋ/: crips who empty their leg bag on the nearest tree

cripmart /krɪpˈmɑrt /: where crips shop for a new body when original one gives up

cripmascot /krɪpˈmæs·kɑt /: a favorite disabled child

cripmasturbation /kripmæs.təˈbeɪ.ʃən/: to play with your own idea of the ownership of sexuality despite disability

cripmating /krɪpˈmeɪt-ɪŋ /: crips having sex with the sole purpose of procreating and making little crips who look just like them

cripmembership /krip/ˈmem.bə.ʃɪp/: to be accepted in the disability community

cripmigration /krɪpˈmaɪ·greɪ·ʃən /: crips who are forced to move out of their familiar dwellings to seek accessibility

cripmile /krɪpˈmaɪl /: speed by which the roll of a wheelchair is measured

cripmill /krɪpˈmɪl /: sheltered workshops where persons with intellectual disabilities perform repetitive tasks for eight hours every day but get pennies for their work while the system claims to do them a favor

cripmind /krɪpˈmaɪnd /: a person's mind when society perceives it as broken

crip-miranda-rights /krip.mərun.da raɪts /: telling wheelchair users they have the right to remain seated

cripmix /krɪpˈmɪks /: a group of people representing various types of disabilities

cripmobile /krɪpˈmoʊˈbil /: vehicle adapted for specific disabilities

CripMoses /krɪpˈmoʊ·sæz /: crip to first part the sea of social segregation; Ed Roberts

cripmorphing /kripmɔːrfing/: the act of adapting to life with a disability

cripmunk /krɪpˈmʌŋk /: disabled chipmunk

cripmuse /krɪpˈmjuz /: the creative energy of a disabled artist

cripmutation /kripmjuːˈteɪ.ʃən/: disabilities that are progressive in nature

cripmythology /krɪpˈmɪ·θɑl·ə·dʒi /: almost everything that society thinks about crips

cripnatural /krɪpˈnætʃ.ər.əl/: crips whose disabilities were caused by the aging process

Cripn'go /krɪpˈn.goʊ /: some businesses' idea of claiming compliance by providing minimum access requirements and calling it a go.

cripnip /krɪpˈnɪp /: medical marijuana

cripn'ride /krɪpˈn·raɪd /: some people's practice of sitting on a crip's wheelchair as if it were a toy

cripn'run /krɪpˈn·rʌn /: ringing doorbells with an ablebodied accomplice

cripn'tell /krɪpˈn. tel /: to make out with a crip and then tell your friends about it

Cripnamese /krɪpˈnə·miːz /: a crip from Vietnam

cripnamite /krɪpˈnə·maɪt /: a crip with explosive temper

cripnap /krɪpˈnæp /: what crips do when they need rest

cripnival /krɪpˈnə·vəl /: a carnival that celebrates crip beauty in an attempt to heal the wounds left by a history that used people with disabilities as circus shows, panhandlers or other forms of demeaning entertainment

cripnecology /krip.nəˈkɒl.ə.dʒ/: an OBGYN who actually knows women with disabilities can get pregnant and give birth

Cripnochio /krɪpˈpɪn·oʊ·ki·oʊ /: a crip who lies a lot

cripnoculation /krɪpˈnɑk·jəˌleɪ·ʃən /: vaccine against polio

cripnogamy /krɪpˈnɑg·ə·mi /: the practice of staying faithful to one crip

cripnomore /krɪpˈnoʊ·mɔr /: a temporarily disability that has reversed to ablebodiness.

cripnopoly /krɪpˈnɑp·ə·li /: the endless political games played around housing accessibility issues

cripnormality /krɪpˈnɔr·mæl·ɪ·t̪i /: people who grew up disabled

cripnosee /kripno si/: crips whose disabilities are not visible

cripnosis /krɪpˈnəʊ.sɪs /: a crip's personal prognosis of abilities and limitations

Crip O-P

Crip O-P

cripobsession /krɪpəbˈseʃ.ən/: to have a fetish for specific disabilities; devotees

cripoccupied /krɪpˈɑk·jəˌpaɪd /: a busy crip

cripocentric /krɪpˈoʊ·sen·trɪk /: to be seen as arrogant when not allowing non-disabled folks to decide for crips' bodies and lives.

cripochet /krɪpˈəˌʃeɪ /: the ricochet of bad karma that returns to haunt those who made fun of gimpy people

cripocricy /krɪpˈɑk·rə·si /: the act of building ramps and painting parking spaces but denying disabled people the right to own their lives

cripofilic /krɪpˈoʊ·fɪl·ɪk /: people whose hearts bleed at the sight or thought of a disabled person

cripogenous /krɪpˈ ɒdʒ·ɪ·nəs /: a crip's erogenous zones of nontraditional nature

Cripohontas /kripo.ka.hon.tas/: a Native American crip

cripoke /krɪpˈoʊk /: the act of poking crips on parts of the body they can't feel

cripolitician /kripˌpɒl.ɪˈtɪʃ.ən/: crips who run for public office seeking the vote of the crip community but lack an agenda addressing the needs and lives of people with disabilities

cripolo /krɪpˈoʊ·loʊ /: Italian term of affection for crips

cripology /krɪpˈɑl·ə·dʒi /: the study of crip culture

cripolulu /krɪpˈoʊ·luː·luː /: crips' dreams of Hawaii

cripometer /krɪpˈɒm.ɪ.tər /: instrument used to measure the discomfort of ablebodied people around crips

criponality /krɪpˈənˈæl.ə.t̬i /: as to having strong crip personality

cripondering /krɪpˈan·dər·ɪŋ /: to wonder about one's disability

criponnence /krɪpˈoʊ·nsəns /: a crip's sexual innocence

criponomics /krɪpˈə·nam·ɪks /: crips living on fixed incomes

Cripopatra /krɪpˈoʊ·pæt·ræ /: historical crip beauty with whom every man fell in love

cripopolis /krɪpˈap·ə·lɪs /: big city where crips reside

cripoppotamus /krɪpˈə·paʈ·ə·məs /: disabled hippo

criporation /krɪpˈə·reɪ·ʃən /: corporation ran by crips

crip-ornament /krip ˈɔː.nə.mənt /: to choose physically attractive crips to advertise a product or event

cripornication /krɪpˈɔː.nɪ.keɪ.ʃən /: crips who fornicate without guilt

criportation /krɪpˈɔrt·eɪ·ʃən /: the deportation of undocumented crips

criportreat /krɪpˈɔr.trit /: what crips do on Halloween

criportunistic /krɪpˈər·tu·nɪst·ik /: person who sees crips as an easy target or an opportunity for an easy lay

criposexual /krɪpˈoʊˌsek·ʃu·əl /: crips who feel attracted to other crips of the same gender

cripostrophe /krɪpˈosˈtrə.fi /: a crip's way of owning our disability

cripotato /krɪpˈə·teɪ·t̪oʊ /: a crip that has been dropped

cripothermia /krɪp ·pəˈθɜr·mi·ə/: what happens to crips after extreme exposure to social indifference

cripottle /krɪpˈɑt̪·əl /: spicy Latin crip

crip-pack /krɪpˈpæk /: wild crips who travel together and hunt ablebodied people

crippadre /krɪpˈɑ:·dreɪ /: disabled priest

crip-pasa /krɪp pæs·æ /: Spanish crip term for "What's up?!"

crip-perception /krip pəˈsep.ʃən /: people who are perceived as being disabled but aren't

cripperina /krɪpˈə·ri·nə /: disabled ballerina

crip-permit /krip /pəˈmɪt /: disability parking tag

cripperupper /krɪp-pər ˈʌp·ər /: a cheerful crip

crip-pick /krɪpˈpɪk /: the act of choosing the least disabled people to represent inclusiveness in a place that claims equality

CrippleA /krɪpˈeɪ /: towing service for broken down wheelchairs

cripplectomy /krɪp·əlˈek·tə·mi /: to eliminate the possibility of conceiving a child with a disability

cripplelicious /krɪp·əlˈlɪʃ·əs /: a delicious crip

cripplesapians /krɪp·əlˈsæp·i·enz /: crips belonging to the human race

crippletarian /krɪp·əlˈ teər·i·ən /: those who prefer to eat crips and find them to be delicious

cripplemunication /kripkəˌmjuː.nɪˈkeɪ.ʃən/: American Sign Language

CrippleX /krɪpˈeks /: X-Rated crip material

cripportunity /krɪpˈər·tu·nɪ·t̬i /: what Walmart thinks it provides by hiring disabled workers as greeters and bypassing them when hiring for higher positions.

cripPresident /krɪpˈrez·ɪ·dənt /: FDR

crip-preventable /krip prɪˈven.tə.bl̩ /: disabilities that could have been avoided

crip-prevention /krɪpˈrɪ·ven·ʃən /: the March of Dimes

crip-procreation /krip prəʊ.kriˈeɪ.ʃən/: crips who have children knowing their disability could be inherited

crip-prosperity /krip prɒsˈper.ɪ.ti /: crips who are able to get out of receiving government benefits and make it on their own

crip-proxy /krip ˈprɒk.si/: nondisabled individuals who serve on boards which have decision making power over the lives of those with disabilities

cripublican /krip pʌb.lɪ.kən/: crips who vote against their own best interest

crippuns /krɪpˈʌns /: intellectual play with words using disability as the punch line

Crip Q-R-S

Crip Q-R-S

cripquake /krɪpˈkweɪk /: spastic person having an orgasm

CripQuayle /krɪpˈkweɪl /: crip who doesn't know how to spell the word potato

cripquest /krɪpˈkwest /: a disabled person's search of self

cripqueer /krip/kwɪər/: non heterosexual crips who are open and proud of their sexuality

cripquila /krɪpˈkiˑlə /: crip on tequila

cripquilt /krɪpˈkwɪlt /: a quilt especially made to fit over the legs of a wheelchair user

cripquitecture /krɪpˈkɪˌtekˑtʃər /: the building of ramps

crip-ratification /kripræt.ɪ.fɪˈkeɪ.ʃən//: the ratification of disability human rights at the global level; the CRPD

criprear /krɪpˈrɪər /: the delicate buttocks of a roller

cripredemption /krip/rɪˈdemp.ʃən/: crips' ability to forgive their bodies for failing them

cripregret /krip rɪˈgret /: crips who suddenly realize they've wasted their time being angry instead of living fully

crip-reinvention /krip͵riː.ɪnˈventʃən/: crips who spell the word crip with a "k"

crip-rental /krɪpˈren·təl /: the practice of using fake disabled models to promote products used by people with real disabilities.

crip-remote-control /krip /rɪˈməʊt kənˈtrəʊl /: crips whose disabilities require legal guardianship

criprevival /krip/ /rɪˈvaɪ.vəl/: a disability prayer group that does not focus on healing the body but on resurrecting the spirit

criprevenge /krip/rɪˈvendʒ/: crips who turn around and prove others wrong after having been told they would never accomplish something

criprevolution /krip ˌrev.əˈluː.ʃən/ : birth of the Disability Rights Movement

criprewind /krɪpˈri�·wɑɪnd /: memories of pre-crip days

CripRex /krɪpˈreks /: crips known for their abnormally short arms

criprhythm /krɪpˈrɪð·əm /: the way crips move to music

criprib /krip /rɪb/ : supposedly Adam's rib after it was removed for the making of Eve

criprising /krip ˈraɪ.zɪŋ/: crip in an elevator which is moving up

crip-ripening /krip ˈraɪ.pəning/ : older crips

CripRock /krɪpˈrɒk /: crip version of Chris Rock

criprodeo /krɪpˈroʊ·diˌoʊ /: yearly event where ablebodied people try to tame wild motorized wheelchairs while crips cheer

criprotica /krip /ɪˈrɒt.ɪ.kə /: disability focused erotic material that does not place emphasis on the pity approach but on the fact that people with disabilities are also sexual beings

criprole /kriprəʊ/: social expectations of how crips should behave

criprophecy /krɪpˈrɑf·ə·si /: the unavoidable truth that every person will eventually join the crip community through the aging process.

criprrender /krɪpˈren.dɚ /: what happens when an ablebodied person surrenders to a passionate crip lover

criprunning /krɪpˈ rʌn·ɪŋ /: Forrest Gump

cripsack /krɪpˈsæk /: slang for a crip's sleeping quarters or space where intimacy takes place

cripsake /krɪpˈseɪk /: something you keep to remember a crip friend

cripsalt /krɪpˈsɔlt /: a crip's sweat and tears

cripsaw /krɪpˈsɔ /: report of something seen by a crip

cripscandal /krip ˈskæn.dəl/ : disabilities that were acquired under scandalous circumstances; Larry Flint

cripscene /krɪpˈsin /: anything crips do in public

cripscrewed /krip /skrudː/: when crips' mobility aids fail

cripschool /kripskuːl/: a school of catfish who think they're dogs

cripscoop /krip/: wheelchair lifts

cripsecret /krɪpˈsiˑkrɪt /: the fact that all crips have once wished they weren't disabled

cripservation /krɪpˈsər·veɪ·ʃən /: disabled people's ability to stay whole while the world acts as if they were broken.

cripshame /krip/ʃeɪm/: crips who feel ashamed of having a disability or fear being stared at

cripshape /krɪpˈʃeɪp /: anybody who does not measure up to Barbie and Ken

crip-shortage /krip ˈʃɔː.tɪdʒ /: what some employers claim to be the case when justifying low number of disabled employees

cripshouting /kripˈʃaʊ.tɪŋ/: some people's habit of yelling when trying to communicate with a deaf person as if doing so could make them hear

cripsight /krip/saɪt/: a blind person's guide dog

cripship /krɪpˈʃɪp /: accessible cruise

cripsilence /krɪpˈsaɪ·ləns /: people who hear no evil but see plenty of it /krɪpˈ /: deaf folks

cripsimulation /krip/ˌsɪm.jʊˈleɪ.ʃən/: the use of able-bodied actors to represent life with a disability

crip-sin /krɪpˈsɪn /: anything crips do to defy society's unrealistic asexual assumptions of disability

cripsinuate /krip ɪnˈsɪn.ju.eɪt /: to insinuate that somebody has a disability

cripsivility /krɪpˈsɪ.vɪl.ɪ.ti /: crips with visible disabilities

cripslap /krɪpˈslæp /: involuntary spasm that hits a person on the face

cripslut /kripˈslʌt/: label given to a crip who decides to be sexually assertive

cripsmear /krɪpˈsmɪər /: the use of demeaning language towards people with disabilities

cripspecial /krɪp speʃ.əl /: two crips for the price of one

cripspell /krɪpˈspel /: the inability to stop staring at a disabled person

cripsphere /krɪpˈsfɪər /: poetic way of saying wheel

cripspit /krɪpˈspɪt /: crip slam poet

cripspiritual /krɪp ˈspɪr.ɪ.tju.əl /: crips who deal with their disability through religion

cripsplash /krɪp/splæʃ/: a disabled mermaid

cripstrument /krɪp.strə.mənt/: a crip's tongue

cripspook /krɪpˈspuk /: to be shocked by a disabled person's average normality

cripspooning /krɪpˈspuːn-ɪŋ /: snuggling with a lover whose body doesn't quite fit in the usual snuggling positions

cripspot /krɪpˈspɑt /: popular hang out with cheap drinks and accessible restrooms

cripstack /krɪpˈstæk /: crip sex in the missionary position

cripstalling /krɪpˈstɔl·ɪŋ /: delaying the news of irreversible disability to a new crip

cripstamina /krɪpˈstæm·ə·nə /: how long a crip's erection can last

cripstarter /krɪpˈstɑrt̬·ər /: caffeine

cripstate /krɪpˈsteɪt /: a state of feeling disabled even though you're not

cripstatistic /krɪpˈstə·tɪs·tɪk /: numbers assigned to crips so it becomes easier to speak of them in the third person

cripsterectomy /krɪpstərˈek.tə.mi/: the sterilization of crips who, society believes, should not procreate; the "Ashley Treatment"

cripsteer /krɪpˈstɪər /: the way crips move the wheel of a vehicle

cripstereo /krɪpˈster·iˌoʊ /: the ability to clearly hear what a crip is saying

cripsticles /krɪpˈstɪ·kəls /: testicles of a crip

cripstinctive /krɪpˈstɪŋk·tɪv /: a crip's natural instinct to try to do things on his /her own

cripstinguish /krɪpˈstɪŋ·gwɪʃ /: an ablebodied person's ability to distinguish one crip from another

cripstink /krɪpˈstɪŋk /: a disabled skunk

cripstitution /krɪpˈstɪ·tu·ʃən /: a crip's oldest profession

Cripstock /krɪpˈstɑːk /: global gathering of crip artists of all genres of art and of all ages of expression.

cripstop /krɪpˈstɑp /: what crips do when they have to empty their bladder or bag

cripstorage /kripstɔːr.ɪdʒ/: facilities that house crips who get left and forgotten; nursing homes

cripstork /krip/stɔːk/: stork that delivers disabled babies

cripstorm /krɪpˈstɔrm /: the explosive emotions of a crip who is coming to terms with the permanence of disability

cripstory /krɪpˈstɔː.ri /: history of crip activism

cripstraight /krɪpˈ streɪt/: a crip who is not gay

cripstray /krip/streɪ/: homeless crip

cripstrip /krɪpˈstrɪp /: sexy crip stripping for a lover

cripstruck /kripstrʌk/: initial shock when meeting somebody you did not expect to be disabled

cripstructure /krɪpˈstrʌk·tʃər /: an accessible building

cripstuck /krɪpˈstʌk /: a roller stuck in the sand or the snow

cripstunt /krɪpˈstʌnt /: to make others believe you're disabled and then laugh about it

cripstupidity /krɪpstuˈpɪd·ɪ·t̬i/: Social Security Administration's practice of asking people with permanent and irreversible disabilities if they're still disabled

cripsuality /krɪpˈsjʊəl.ə.ti /: socially misunderstood sensuality exuding from a crip's body and mind

cripsualization /krɪpˈʒu·əl·aɪz·eɪ.ʃən /: the act of imagining crips naked

cripsuccess /krɪpˈsək·ses /: a disabled person's ability to find a job

cripsult /krɪpˈsʌlt /: the use of the word crip by a non disabled person.

cripsuperhero /krip suː.pər hɪə.rəʊ / Super Man

cripsupial /krɪpˈsu·pi·əl /: crip parent
with infant

cripsurprise /krɪpsəˈpraɪz/ : crips who
get pregnant after they had been told they
could never conceive

Crip T–U

Crip T–U

criptaboo /krɪpˈtə·bu /: sex and disability in the same sentence

criptachio /krɪpˈtæʃ·iˌoʊ /: pistachio tasting crip

criptaco /krɪpˈtɑ·koʊ /: some men's definition of a crip woman's vagina

crip-tac-toe /krɪpˈtæk·toʊ /: crips aligned in rows of four

criptake /krɪpˈteɪk /: to participate in disability related events

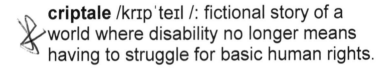**criptale** /krɪpˈteɪl /: fictional story of a world where disability no longer means having to struggle for basic human rights.

criptalistic /krɪpˈtəl.ɪst.tɪk /: being realistic about one's disability

criptalize /krɪpˈtəl.aɪz /: to explain ourselves clearly to a non disabled person

Criptanamera /krɪpˈtæn·ə·meər·ə /:
 popular crip Latin song

criptastic /krɪpˈtæs·tɪk /: a fantastic crip
or situation

criptatious /krɪpˈteɪ.ʃəs /: a flirtatious crip

criptaught /krɪpˈ tɔt /: ablebodied
people's political correctness as learned
from crips

criptaunt /krip/tɔːnt/: to fuck with the
hopes of persons with disabilities by
offering services that only exist on paper

criptease /krɪpˈtiz /: the medical
industry's idea of making those things that
are essential to crips' ability to function so
out of reach that no crip can afford it.

criptellect /krɪpˈtəlˌekt /: a crip's intellect
and psyche

Criptember /krɪpˈtem·bər /: charitable actions by ablebodied people towards the crip community during the months September, November and December

criptemple /krɪpˈtem·pəl /: the disabled body

criptenna /krɪpˈten·ə /: a crip's ability to detect the presence of a kindred crip

criptense /krɪpˈtens /: suspense experienced in the anticipation of a blind date with a crip

criptentional /krip /ɪnˈten.ʃən.əl/ : to purposely run over a walking person's toes

criptepenneur /krɪpˈte·pen·nɜːr /: crip who owns his or her body

cripterosexual /krɪpˈt̠ər·ə·sek·ʃu·əl /: to like crips of the opposite sex

cripterpretation /krɪpˈtɜr·prɪˈteɪ·ʃən /: the way crips interpret the reactions of nondisabled people

cripthanasia /krɪpˈθəˈneɪ·ʒə /: the believe that people with disabilities are better off dead; abortion of a fetus believed to have a disability; the killing of government funds destined to assist people with disabilities

cripthis /krɪpˈðɪs /: a crip's way of saying "Fuck You"

cripthru /krɪpˈθru /: a fast food drive thru for motorized wheelchairs

cripticality /krɪpˈtɪ·kæl·ə·ʈi /: practical short cuts in a crip's way of doing certain things

cripticism /krɪpˈtəˌsɪz·əm /: judgmental opinions people with disabilities are exposed to when wanting to assert themselves and own their lives.

cripticulate /krɪpˈtɪk·jə·lət /: a crip's ability to articulate words despite a speech impediment

criptilence /krɪpˈtəl·əns /: the foul smell of injustice towards disabled people

Crip-Tin-Tin /krɪpˈtɪn·tɪn /: disabled dog

criptistic /krɪpˈtɪs.tɪk /: an artistic crip

criptock /krɪpˈtɑːk /: thoughts of a broken clock

criptogenic /krɪpˈə·dʒen·ɪk /: crips who are photogenic

criptographer /krɪpˈţəˌgræf·ər /: photographer who specializes in photographing crips

criptomania /krɪpˈoʊ·meɪ·ni·ə /: the habit of staring at people with disabilities

criptoo /krɪpˈtu /: recognition of one another between crips

criptoones /krɪpˈtuːn /: disability friendly and properly represented cartoons about disabled people

criptop /krɪpˈtɒp /: sexual position where the crip is on top

 Criptopia /krɪpˈtoʊ·pi·ə /: Berkley, CA

Criptorican /krɪpˈphweər·toʊ·ri·kæn /: Jose Feliciano

criptoris /krɪpˈt̪ər·əs /: woman pleasure button in a crip woman's genitalia

criptoversy /krɪpˈtoʊˌvɜr·si /: controversy surrounding the sexual rights of people with cognitive disabilities

criptransport /kripˈtræn.spɔːt/: accessible transportation

criptraining /kripˈtreɪ.nɪŋ/: having to learn how to work with a body that no longer communicates with your brain and/or lifestyle;

criptriplication /kriptrɪp.lɪ. keɪ.ʃən /: multiple crips in the same room

criptrauma /krip/trɔː.mə/: what a person experiences after a sudden disability

criptualistic /krɪpˈtʃ·u·əl·ɪs·tɪk /: a disabled person's daily routine with the body

criptunia /krɪpˈtun·jə /: an exotic flower similar to petunias but with a missing petal

cripunknown /krip/ʌnˈnəʊn/: the origin of disabilities that are still under research

cripturesque /krɪpˈ tʃəˈresk /: crips painted as part of a landscape

cripturnal /krɪpˈtɜr·nəl /: crips who stay up all night

cripty-nine /krip sɪk.sti naɪn /: crips in the 69 sexual position

CripTV /krɪpˈti·vi /: a network that focuses entirely on every aspect of disability life

cripublication /krɪpˈʌb·lɪ·keɪ·ʃən /: New Mobility Magazine

cripunion /kripuː.ni.ən/: marriage between crips

cripundity /krɪpˈʌn.dɪ.ti /: the profundity of a crip's personal experience

Crip V-W-X-Y-Z

Crip V-W-X-Y-Z

cripvine /krip vaɪn/: place where gossip in the disability community is first heard

cripvillain /krɪpˈvɪl·ən /: Captain Hook

cripventive /krip/: practical things cripinvent to make life easier

cripventure /kripˈven.tʃə/: what happens when crips with opposite disabilities hang out and drink

cripvictimization /krɪpˌvɪk.tɪˈmaɪˈzeɪ.ʃən/: negative labels forced upon people with disabilities

cripvultures /kripˈvʌl.tʃərs/: personal injury attorneys

cripwatch /kripwɒtʃ/: able-bodied person who makes sure a crip doesn't drink and roll

cripwave /krɪpˈweɪv /: the polio epidemic

cripwear /krip/weər/: line of clothing for disabled people

cripwhisperer /krɪpˈwɪs.pərer/: counselor or therapist who works with people with disabilities

cripwish /krɪp/wɪʃ/: those who wish they could experience having a disability; crip wannabes

cripwitch /krɪpwɪtʃ/: witch with a broken broom

cripwon't /krɪpˈ woʊnt/: denial about the permanence of a disability

cripxorcism /krɪpˈk.sɔɪ.zəm/: some people's believe that seizure disorders can be expelled out of a person like evil spirits

cripXRay /krɪpˈeks•reɪ /: the naked vulnerability of a crip when he/she is stared at in public

Cripzilla /krɪpˈzɪlə /: fictional disabled person of ferocious nature

cripzoo /krɪpˈzu/:   Polio ward back in the fifties; institutions where people with disabilities are contained and visited by religious and/or charitable organizations

cripzoom /krɪp zum/:   society's tendency to overemphasize a crip's obvious differences

About The Author:

Maria R. Palacios is a feminist writer, poet, author, public speaker, polio survivor and spoken word performer who uses the power of her words to empower and educate on issues surrounding disability culture, disability and sexuality and cultural diversity in general. In the artistic world, Maria is known as The Goddess on Wheels.

www.facebook.com/goddessonwheels
palaciosmaria66@gmail.com

Also by Maria R. Palacios:

The Female King
 Publisher: Atahualpa Press
 ISBN-10: 0972648305

Karate on Wheels, A Journey Of Self Discovery
Publisher: Atahualpa Press
ISBN: 9780972648325

Made in the USA
Lexington, KY
19 April 2017